There Stood Our Dog

Written by Anne Houghton Illustrated by Craig Smith

On Tuesday, Mum opened the front door and there stood our dog.

"How did she get out?" asked Mum.

Our backyard has fences all around it
and two tall gates.
How did she get out?

We checked the fences.
There were no holes.
We checked the gates.
They were locked.

On Wednesday, when I came out of school,
there stood our dog.
How did she get out?

We checked the fences.
There were no holes.
We checked the gates.
They were locked.

On Thursday, Mum asked me to buy some milk.
When I came out of the shop,
there stood our dog.
How did she get out?

We checked the fences.
There were no holes.
We checked the gates.
They were locked.

On Friday, our neighbour
brought us some apples from his tree.

He rang the doorbell.
When Mum answered it,
there stood our dog, next to our neighbour.

“How did she get out again?” asked Mum.

Mum checked the fences.
There were no holes.
She checked the gates.
They were still locked.

We decided to work out a plan.

On Saturday, when everyone was home,
we all hid in the backyard
to watch our dog.

My sister hid behind a tree.
Dad hid in the shed,
and watched through the window.
Mum hid in the playhouse next to the trampoline.
I hid on the shed roof, with Dad's binoculars.

We waited and waited.
We watched and watched.
Nothing happened.

Our dog lay in the sun next to her kennel all day.
We got tired of waiting.
We got tired of watching.

We went inside.
How did she get out every day?
Did she dig under the fence?
Did someone open the gates?

On Sunday, we found out.
Again we waited and watched.

Squeak, squeak went the springs
of our trampoline next to the back fence.
Bounce, bounce went our dog
as she leapt up and down
and up, up, over the fence.

So that's how she got out!

Our next plan was to move the trampoline.